Mournful Lover

Jazmin Galloway

Copyright © 2023 by Jazmin Galloway

All rights reserved.

978-1-7351652-8-8

LCN: 2023913465

No portion of this book may be reproduced in any form without written permission from the publisher or author, except as permitted by U.S. copyright law.

Mentions of
   ~Self-harm
~Domestic Violence
~Self-hate
~Toxic relationships
~Sexual content

To those who don't forget.

Even though I let you know me...

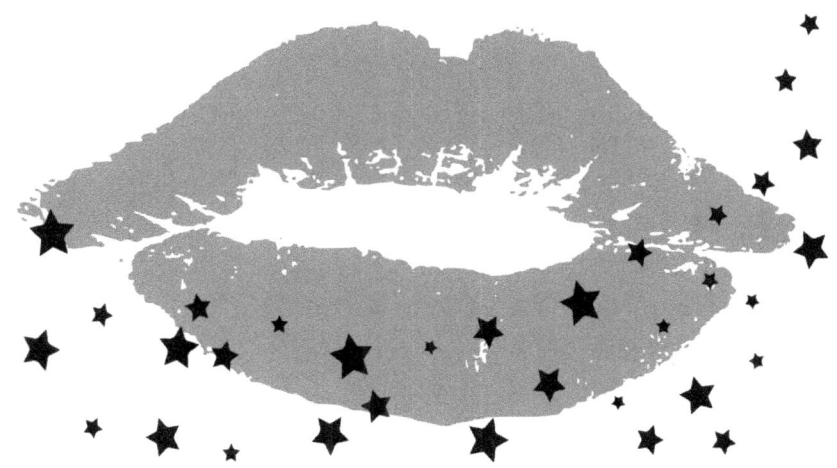

THE THOUGHT OF LOVE tastes so sweet
　Like ice cream on a summer day

Hot want floods the blood
Cooled by a summer's breeze

I used to want love so bad
I dreamed of how it looked
Shaking hands and trembling lips
Tight hugs and midnight's kiss

Love looked so fragile
And yet so true
Pure, and kind
Docile, demure

Love looked like babies breath
Calling all emotion unconditionally
Sprouting lies that sound so neat
Rewriting a person's history

I wanted to love so bad
I let it take control of me
Looking through rose-tented lenses
Seeking a lack of misery

But even that love
So sickly sweet
Came to a burning end

For all the love that I received
   I gave it back tenfold
   Because love to me
   Is more valuable than gold

   But all the love I have received
   Has only filled me so
   Just a little drip of it
   And I turn to snow

   Melting on your cracked pavement
   And splashed into your sneakers

   Run over by fate's cruel reign
   And tied to societies speakers

   Blaring loud warnings across the sky
   That my kind of love is not enough

   That soft whispers,

And even softer hands

Isn't the right kind of love

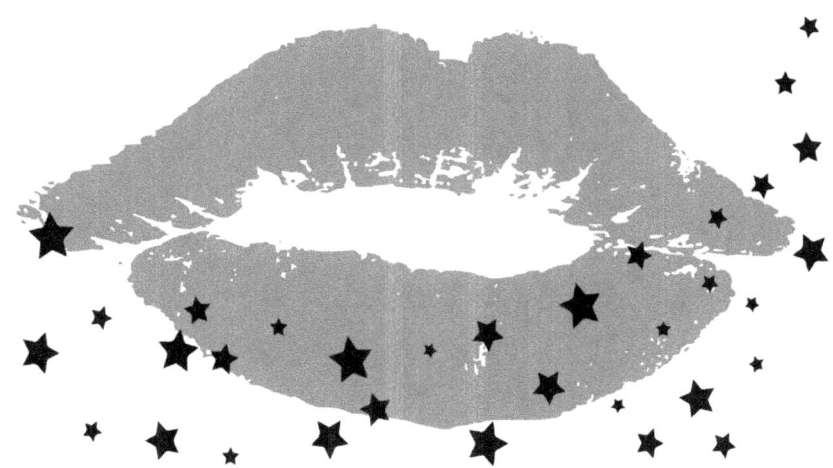

I RUN AWAY FROM all my insecurities
Instead of facing them head on

All that learning, and practicing
To fight my demons
Has made me headstrong

This is a battle I can't win
In my Adidas and high-waist leggings
My crop top isn't armor
and protects me naught from all the begging

'Just come talk to me'
They say
'How old are you?'
They ask
'You're so beautiful'
They comment
'I want you'
They demand

But I don't want them
It's their deep-set eyes
And hard, grip, hands

That scare me away
And seek me out

While I'm screaming

I don't want you

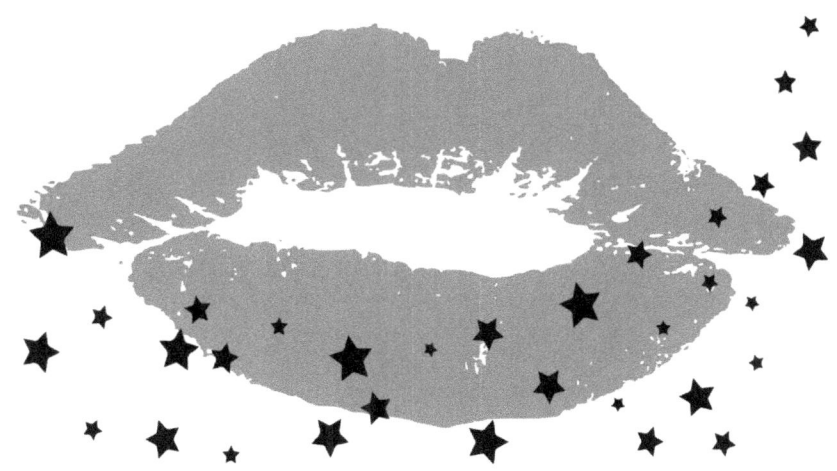

Dark eyes reflect the earth
Light eyes reflect the sea

Dark lips respond with sin
Light lips respond with desire

Dark hands create chaos
Light hands create death

All rolled together
In bed

They fuse

Making scary nights alone
Bring tremors to my bones

And cause wet, hot, streaks of emotion
Down my face and off my chin

I wonder what the earth sees in my sin, is it chaos?

Or what the sea sees in my desire, is it death?

I wonder why hands age my face
When they touch me so tenderly
And why hot bodies make me burn
When there is no fire next to me

All it is
Is cold lust
Balled into a pretty package
Signed love

S̲o̲ ̲b̲o̲l̲d̲l̲y̲ I lie
    About who I am
    Or how I act

    So your image of me is
    Perfect
    And I am all you need

    But I am not,
    So far detached from you
    It burns to reveal myself

    Pull back my layers
    Which make you cry
    And show off the seed I still am

    Cause I have not grown
    Not without the water from your tears
    Or the sun's rays reflected in your eyes
    Not without your dirt filled hands

Covering me
Endlessly

I AM DEPENDENT
   On your validation
   That I am doing well

   I am dependent
   On your praise
   That I am doing well

   I am dependent
   On your well-being
   To fail so I may care for you

   I am dependent
   On your scars
   So that I may repair you

   Toxic in my own mind
   Because I care so much

   For deeper conversation

And even deeper touch

Loaded whispers
And hurried kisses
In a warm room and cold bed

So when your heat touches mine
I don't burst into fire

Like my religion said

When I'm with you

Unwed
To anything
But your heart

M<small>Y FIRST PROMISE</small>
  Is not a promise
  But a half-truth

  My expectation of my capabilities
  Is more than I can ever do

  So I don't lie
  But forget to say

  That no promises mean
  Take it anyway

  Take my words at face value
  So I can value your face
  Your lips
  Your hips and the way they move
  To me, on me, through me

  Like water in the sea,

Harmonize with my design
And criticize my every being

Because I love the way you hurt me
And make sick
To be myself
In love with you

Put an H on your chest
  And handle it
  Is what my father said

  Those words have kept me steady
  And balance my much too large head

  So that light promises don't wrinkle the sheets
  On my bed
  And the unvalued don't get a chance
  to be bred
  Not be me
  Who has her shit together
  In theory

M<small>Y DREAM LOVE</small>
   Isn't the only love I crave

   At least I know the difference
   But that's what makes this so hard

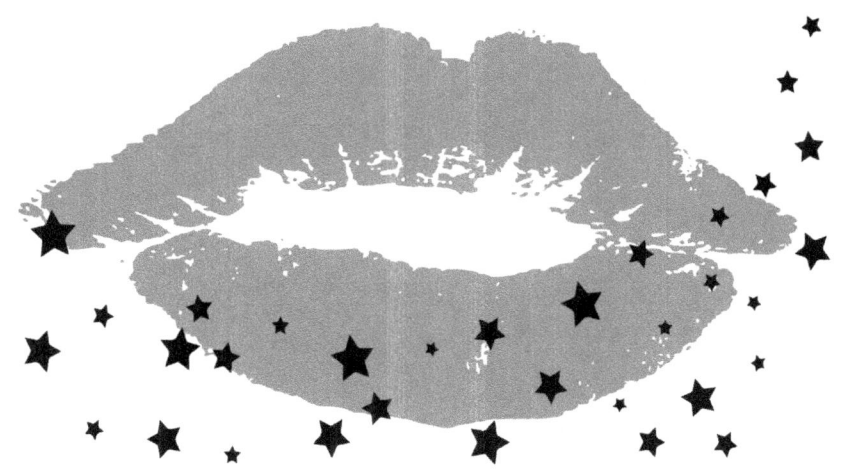

FORMED BY MY EXPERIENCE
Influenced by my environment

I have grown into the woman I am
With some semblance of who I hope to be

And she is I
And I am her

With the same round face
And exuberant words

Her life is a movie
That I directed
But when I reflect it
I wind up rejected
And dejected
And misplaced

By the same hands

That wrote the story
In the first place

For all I know
it is right in front of me

That painful love
I seek
That cuts me so deep
I bleed

But not externally
But internally

So that I hear the blood go whoosh
And my beating heart slowly fills
with the dirt from the earth

As they bury me in my current state
Expecting and wanting
But doing nothing to get

I pray my results reflect my effort
Because life is a mirror from past to present
And present to future
And me is all I see
In the mirror of life

WHEN I DREAM OF them

    I see slender eyes that are dark like mine
    And a crooked smile that makes me swoon

    With hands that cover mine and hide them away
    So I can't see the marks of my doom

    To fall endlessly in those dough born eyes
    And deeply into those open arms

    And ride the high of true love's kiss
    And taste the fruit of true love's charms

    When I dream of me

    I am black with strife
    Bled by life
    Cut with a knife
    That I was holding

Drinking poison
To make me numb
Holding guns
With shaking thumbs
And wheezing lungs

Until it all goes black
Then white
As I rise over life
And disappear
Like I was never here

I GUESS MY SKULL is the same color as popcorn
   That's why it cracks so often
   And leaks out a buttery substance
   That wets my coffin

   I guess my heart's made of aluminum
   That's why it's so easy to crumble
   So easy to tear apart
   The interaction makes me humble

   I guess my body's made of paper
   That's why I rip myself to shreds
   And fall in pieces on the ground
   For other's to make their beds

   I guess my words are full of salt
   That's why they make other's wince
   The words I say hurt deeply
   Evil is so easy to convince

I'M LIKE A SHIRT
   That's been sweat on
   And wore to threads

   So that my seams smell like you
   And remind you of better days

   Where you didn't have responsibility
   Or bills, and artillery

   Where you were young and dumb
   Sometimes didn't wash
   So you could keep wearing
   Your favorite shirt

I USED TO LOVE your voice
    The deep rasp was so enticing
    Like fingers through my tangled hair
    And the vibrator in my nightstand

    You were my vibrator
    Bringing momentary pleasure
    And long term shame

    That I rubbed my hands so raw
    They bring me no pleasure to gain

    In your deep rasps, I found purchase
    That my desire could be fulfilled
    But your ever-changing moods
    Brought disdain to my thrill
    And I no longer found you

    In love
    With me

Because you never were

My eyes bleed red roses
   That decorate your coffin

   You swear I put you there
   That it was my chalk drawn in
   Your shape
   Your form
   Your body
   On uneven concrete

   That I made you splinter
   Shatter
   And break

   That it was my wood
   That cracked your skull
   And lay your memories on the street

   But even my memory is foggy
   From the smoke of your lips

The hum of your mournful weeps
As the night gave in

I think it's hard to realize
That I am you
On the ground
And in the dirt
Six feet deeper
In the hole of loving myself
And hating what I've become

I'VE SLIPPED OFF MY gloves
  So that I may feel you breathing
  On my skin
  Through your nose

  So unconsciously
  Unaware
  I am here
  Watching you

  Checking to make sure you're breathing

  That your heart is still beating

  Even when your with me

  Unguarded and asleep

  I'm bound to think it's weird
  That you haven't left

So scarred by my own experience
I make plans to push you away

So that I am never as unguarded
As you are now

Weak
And
Unbeknownst
To the evil in me

Who's ready to see

How far we can go

Before we break each other

I KEEP THINKING ABOUT what I've accomplished

And how many swipes it takes to find my ideal self
And how many likes it takes until I like myself
And how many pipes it takes
Before the vehicle of my life breaks down

Into atoms

And I fade into the universe

Which I hope is as vast as they say
So that I don't hurt you
Anymore than I have

You being me
And me being I
And I being just another letter
In the man-made alphabet
So I could talk to U and not you

But instead me

I've confused myself
But I guess I was never clear about *her* anyway

MAYBE IF I PRAY
   I'll be given an answer

   And the words of my poetry
   Will reveal my mistakes

   So that I fix them
   Instead of covering them up

   again

BUT MAYBE NOT

I WONDER IF THE poison I drank was fresh
    If it's taste was a reflection of broken things
    From broken people
    By broken people

    If I brewed it myself
    In a past life
    And sent it to the future
    Because I knew
    I'd mess up so bad

    That I thought ending it was better
    Than living through it

    I wonder if the ink on my paper has dried
    That I am done writing my own story
    Because I waited too long
    And my pages have turned yellow

    I wonder about many things about myself

And no one else
But swear I'm ready to share
All my little things
And cracks and pieces

But really I'm just eager
To stop thinking
About myself
For once

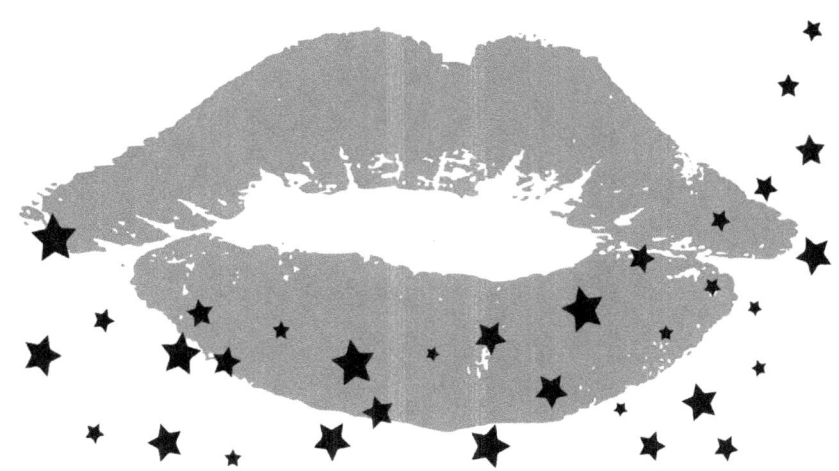

Sometimes I think a baby will change it
   It being me
   Because I feel less than human
   When I push my problems on others
   Especially those who know no better but to love me
   Unconditionally

   Sometimes I crave the attention
   Of platonic love
   That can end so suddenly
   That I lose my breath
   And fall to my knees
   And weep deeply from my breast

   Sometimes I crave the attention
   Of romantic love
   So it can shake me
   So hard that I cannot stand
   And I fall to my knees
   And pray deeply from my breast

Sometimes I crave the attention
Of sexual love
So it can hit me
Like of ton of bricks
And I fall to my knees
And submit to it

Sometimes I think that love will change me
But never consider loving myself
Because it is too powerful
And too scary
And too hard to control

I WISH I WOULD learn that not all love
    Is physical
    So I can stop craving touch
    I don't want
    Or need
    Or feel
    Even when it happens

    I wish I would learn that love I can't see
    Is mental
    And emotional
    So I can stop craving touch
    I don't want
    And don't need
    And can't feel
    Even when it happens

I'VE SPENT TOO MUCH time here
  In my heart
  To not know what it wants
  Or who
  And why

  All that time stays lodged in my throat
  So that I choke
  And struggle
  And move
  Until my neck turns purple
  And I stop struggling
  So time can move again
  Past me

  And my grievances

I'VE KNOWN SOCIETY HATES my skin
   Though they imitate it
   And initiate it

   In their dark room
   With secret chants
   They don't teach you in school

   Hot breath
   And rough strokes
   And closed eyes
   That dream things they'd never admit

   Not to me
   For they think it'll
   Big my head
   And stroke my ego

   But I don't care
   We don't care

Lust is only a part of you
It doesn't have to consume you
Unless you let it
And you like it that way

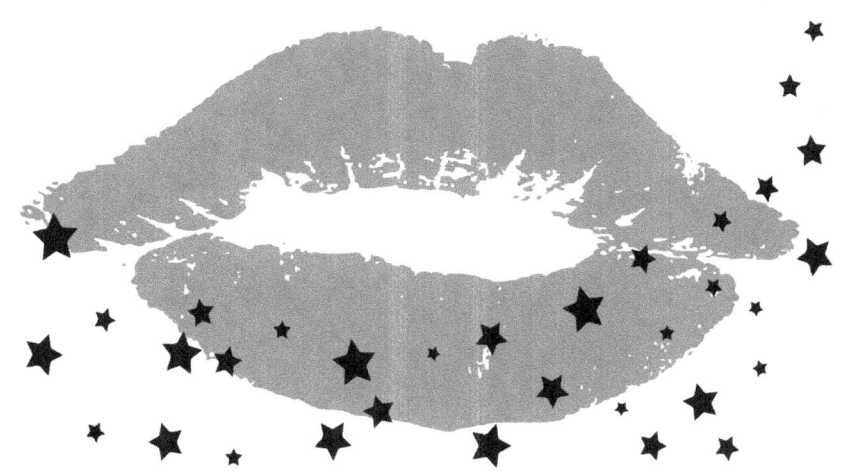

Sometimes I like it that way

SUBTLE LOOKS
    Have never been enough
    To catch my attention

    I'm too stubborn
    To think that it's for me
    To which you look

    Because I don't think I'm good enough
    For your eyes
    So I put more on my plate
    Than I can handle
    And it becomes so heavy
    I drop it

    In front of you
    And you think it's cute
    But I think your laughing
    At me
    And I hate your for it

I hate myself for it

For subtle looks
Have never been enough
To catch your attention

IN MY DREAMS YOU kiss my pulse
   Through my wrist
   And look up through long lashes

   Your lips are sweet like candy
   And your tongue tastes like tea

   Your cologne is too spicy for me
   But I like it, how over powering
   Is your presence

   I am agreeable
   And you steer our ship

   I am submissive
   And you guide our lives

   I am wanton
   And you fulfill our desires

You and I
Me and You

Until death do us part

But only in my dreams
Where you remained locked away
So that I don't have to face reality
Right now

I AM FOREVER INDEBTED to my fantasies

YOU ARE MY LIGHT
  and I love you
  Like still water
  In a half filled cup
  And leftovers
  In a cold fridge

  Because I love you like cooked food
  As my dad says

  Because words from my father
  Are invaluable
  And infinite

  So I share them
  With your seed

  Because
  They are
  Invaluable

And infinite

Weird is a word I invite
Because normal has a bad connotation

Strange is too strong
Unique is too weak

They tell you you're unique
And they say that so is everyone else
So what makes you special,
If we all are

They call you strange
If you don't fit into their version of normal
But since abnormal is rude
Than strange you become

When they call you normal
You have so much anger
Because you are trying your best
Like everyone else

And have nothing special to show for it
Like everyone else

And therefore

You're normal
Not matter how much you hate
It's connotation

But when you're weird
You can be liked or disliked
With no in-between
Or room for promotion
Or demotion
Because you are just
Weird
And that's okay

Because we are too
All of us are weird to someone

Because life is full of
judgment
&
interpretations
&
opinions

My life is full of
  Judgment
  Interpretations
  Opinions

  About myself
  About others

  And I think I've finally found my flaw
  Until it multiples
  And multiples
  And I realized that I have a problem with
  Everything
  About myself
  Except for those few things
  I focus on
  And obsess over
  To the point that I know nothing more
  Then what I work for
  And not a thing about myself

Who am I in the eyes of myself
Except for the one who writes
And speaks to herself more than
Anyone on this earth

I AM NOT
The woman I want to be

Sometimes I think I would be better off as a man
Because I am more masculine
And dominant
And independent
Of societies normal woman

I don't want to be a normal woman
Even if I appreciate all she is
I don't want to be someone other than myself

But it's hard to know what is me
And what is them
Influencing
Me
And my
Woman

My femininity
Is running
From my
Masculinity

But I'm just ignoring myself
And wondering why
It is so hard
To love me

Have you heard my lover
   They sound like wind
   Because they are not there

   Not in the sense where other can hear
   The mournful whispers
   They speak into my ear
   Or the soft sobs
   The place in my throat
   Or the cold winds
   They breathe down my back

   You can't hear my lover
   Because even the wind
   Can not encapsulate
   The emptiness
   They leave behind

THE WORDS I WISH to say to you
    Are engraved on my tombstone

    'Here lies, all I was
    And all I will ever be
    So please accept that
    Before I die, and not just
    after'

    It's up to you to listen
    Understand
    React

    So I'll help you

    Here is my heart without
    I will bled out my chest and die
    So put it back before I do

    Here are my lungs

If you squeeze them hard enough
I'll gasp trying to breathe
And when you let them go they
Expand like a balloon

Here is my brain
If you drop it
I'll forget you
So don't put it up to high, or it might fall
And don't put it too low
Or you may step on it
And crush my life under toe

Here are my emotions
Intangible
But yes, still there
Do what them what you will
But like Play-Doh
Too much playing,
And they will dry up

I'VE TASTED THE FEAST that is a crush
   So much to eat but still not enough
   My mouth waters for the main meal
   And the desert that comes after

   And to wash it down I drink
   The figments of our little interaction

   I've tasted the feast that is heartbreak
   Full of sponge, and fat
   Bones, and slabs
   Of everything that you promise
   But did not pull through

   I've tasted the feast of my expectation
   So rotund and well fed
   That it makes my head spin
   And shoulders droop
   And drag on the floor
   So heavy is the heart

In me

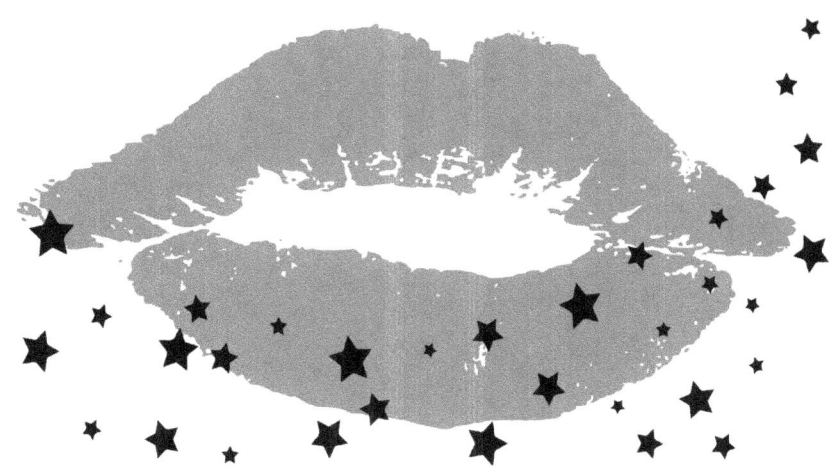

I'VE SAMPLED THE TASTE of your flesh
   And it tastes like the sea
   And it smells like cake
   Yum enough to bite
   And ick enough to hate

   I fear you love my attention to detail
   How I do that thing that makes your eyes roll
   And you limbs curl
   How I say that thing that makes your heart flutter
   And you speak in tongues

   I fear my attention to detail
   But what's been done
   Is done

I'M PERSONALLY OFFENDED BY your success
  When I am suffering
  Without you
  But I know to grow alone
  This is what I have to do

  Suffer
  Experience
  Recover
  And heal well
  So that I can move on

  And never look back
  Even when your voice calls
  Your eyes call
  Your body calls

  I move on
  I recover
  And never look back

IN A MOMENT OF weakness
   I succumb to my fantasy

   I am lost in a shadow of my dreams
   Walking on cloudless air
   And flapping the wings of my heart
   To reach
   You

   It is the pitter patter of asteroids against my head
   that makes me look up

   I have left behind all I know
   To fall

   And so fall I do
   Into the void of unknown
   That is sharing my heart
   With you

I AM SHARING MY heart with you

>To me the purpose of life is to reproduce
>And give back whole heartily into the earth
>That gives to us
>So that our continuation of life creates harmony
>And balance
>
>I feel our communication
>And collaboration
>Is the detonation
>To the bomb of death
>That creates hysteria
>And chaos
>In our own families
>
>We take more than ourselves
>When our veins bleed onto those hardwood floors
>
>We take more than ourselves

When those words stab so deeply it comes out the other side

We take more than ourselves
When it all goes numb, and then all goes black

A piece of me is inside of you
And I take that
When I leave
And you take that
When you leave

So let's stop leaving
It's getting painful

My command of words
   does not apply in speech
   I fumble over my own tongue
   As if it is foreign in my mouth

   I've grown accustomed to the stutter I say with simple words
   And the clarity to which I find in poetic jargon

   My illustrious paintings hang only in my head
   So beautiful and yet transparent
   Because I cannot describe myself in them

   My command of affection
   Does not apply in speech
   The timid soliloquy I've written
   Is hard to say
   And it causes confusion
   In those starry eyes
   For I pray

Pray you will look at my heart which I am baring
Hoping that through my stutter
They are hearing
My command of words

I'VE GOT JUST A few words for you
   The man in my heart
   And the woman nearby
   I hope that I make you feel safe
   And you use my shoulder when you cry
   I hope together we grow gray
   Before together we die
   And I want everyday with you
   to feel like the weightlessness
   of the sky

   I've spent many days thinking
   Of what you will be like
   And how we will be together
   But nothing beats the feeling
   Of just being near each other

   I hope my love is not toxic
   Like society says it is
   And that my sin for you can be forgiven

Unlike my religion tells

Thy love for you is not a cold lust
That cannot be shaken
Thy love for you is not a frozen heart
That is easily taken
Thy love for you is not simple words
That can be easily mistaken
Thy love for you is more
Than just love

I TAKE MY TIME
   in
   Practicing my divination
   to
   Control the flow of my life
   Through
   my will

   That something other than me
   Can manipulate
   The outcome
   Of my future

   I am manifesting
   Greatness
   In the form of flesh
   At my side
   With an open heart
   Willing to love
   And explore

My own
Open heart

Out of my future
Comes
The greatest gift
in all existence

Divinity

In the form of flesh
A spirit
In the shape of man

With golden wings
And no face
Bound to protect
And report
All ill will

Up until

My very

Last

Breath

amen

My reoccurring dreams are always the nightmares
  And when I wake
  every detail gets more vivid as if I'm still asleep
  As if my conscious mind must be afraid
  in order to operated properly

  And I am afraid
  Of many things all at once
  So there is no true culprit
  to
  what keeps me up at night

  And if there is
  My reoccurring dreams
  haven't told me yet

  Who
  Or
  What
  This culprit may be

Maybe it is me,
Or my past life,
Or figments of forgotten memories

Maybe it is
everything and nothing
at once

Maybe
I am reading to far into my hazy, sleep-filled mind
But I can't help letting those dreams guide my consciousness
Because I want to know
Why all my dreams are nightmares

I'VE LONG SINCE LONGED for peace

> While my body practices pacifism
> my words do not
>
> I am always
> On demon time
> As I like to joke
> With those who understand
>
> And sometimes with those who don't
> They think me mental
> But all is well
> As I know myself better than they know me
>
> I've since longed for revenge
>
> Though my words practice retribution
> My body does not

I am always
On demon time
As I like to joke
With those who understand

And sometimes with those who don't
They think me evil
But all is well
As I know myself better than they know me

I've since longed for love

My heart puts in all the work
While my body and mind do not understand
The gravity of the words spilling from my lips like a waterfall

I am always
Ready for more
Or so I tell myself
When I want to understand
sometimes I don't

I think myself unprepared
But all is well
As I know myself better than I think

I AM A MOURNFUL lover
   But not because I am sad
   Or filled with grief
   From the love that has passed

   I am a mournful lover
   But not because of my pity
   For those who have it worse than I
   And for whose situation's are gritty

   I am a mournful lover
   Because I am full of despair
   Knowing that something cannot come from nothing
   If nothing is all that's there

   There is nothing to love
   Here in my heart
   When I refuse to find love
   Where matter exists

All that matters for me is the dream
Of what I want
And not the reality of what I can have
And I feel deep mourning
For myself

For I am a mournful lover

I AM TOO SELF-AWARE

And it eats me up inside

My awareness is pulling at my pride

For I am so quiet that all I do is observe
And all I observe is myself
And now I don't know my self-worth

Am I worth the self I have
And the love I seek
Am I worth the words given to me in letters
And in secret speech

Conversation with myself have grown stale
Now I seek out other's attention
Conversation with them is too hard
So I force my own conventions

That I am a mournful lover
And that is all I am today

Tomorrow I will observe some more
And fight off my sorrow

But today

I AM A MOURNFUL lover

My past dreams
  Don't fulfill me anymore
  And neither do the people in my past

  I've learned it's okay to let them go

  Now I feel comfortable in my skin
  In my heart
  And in my mind

  For which I mourn
  Those days that I felt
  My love was not enough

I will never let you love me

The Limpid Series
Black Or With Sugar?
Windchimes and Sirens
Murder Bird
Light and Sweet

Other Poetry Collections
~Larceny

JAZMIN GALLOWAY started writing poetry in the third grade. With decades of practice came many life changes, achievements, losses, and mistakes. Galloway uses her life experiences and dreams of life to come, and life that has passed, to inspire her poetry. You can find her on Facebook and Instagram @jazminsbooks

www.ingramcontent.com/pod-product-compliance
Lightning Source LLC
Chambersburg PA
CBHW071252070526
44583CB00017B/2439